earth

THE LIFE OF OUR PLANET

Dr. Mike Goldsmith

Illustrated by Dr. Mark A. Garlick

KINGFISHER
LONDON & NEW YORK

Copyright © Kingfisher 2011
Text copyright © Dr. Mike Goldsmith 2011
Published in the United States by Kingfisher,
175 Fifth Ave., New York, NY 10010
Kingfisher is an imprint of Macmillan Children's Books, London.
All rights reserved.

Distributed in the U.S. by Macmillan, 175 Fifth Ave., New York, NY 10010

Library of Congress Cataloging-in-Publication data has been applied for.

ISBN: 978-0-7534-6625-4

Kingfisher books are available for special promotions and premiums.
For details contact: Special Markets Department, Macmillan, 175 Fifth Ave.,
New York, NY 10010.

For more information, please visit www.kingfisherbooks.com

Printed in China
1 3 5 7 9 8 6 4 2
1TR/0611/WKT/UNTD/157MA

Illustration credits: the background image on pages 6–7 and 38–45 (inclusive) is
from Shutterstock/Anton Balazh; the "five Earth clocks" on pages 44–45 are by Julian Baker
(JBIllustrations); the illustrations on pages 30–35 (inclusive) are by Stuart Jackson-Carter;
all other illustrations are by Dr. Mark A. Garlick.

earth

THE LIFE OF OUR PLANET

KINGFISHER
NEW YORK

Worlds begin

Long ago, the part of the universe where our world would one day be born was a cold, dark place. Great clouds hung silently in space, blocking the light of the stars.

Then there came a moment, more than 4.75 billion years ago, when everything changed: a great and ancient star died in an unimaginably vast explosion. The torrents of energy that were released sent shock waves surging through the clouds, seeding the births of many new stars.

Over time, those stars drifted away from one another, making long journeys through the endless blackness of space. Many, perhaps all of them, were surrounded by families of planets—and on at least one of those planets the conditions were right for a remarkable chain of developments to take place.

That planet was Earth, and this is its story.

The life of a planet

The following pages take you to 15 key moments in the life of Earth. They come from the records of the stars, of the rocks, and of human history. Reading these records opens the gateway to the past and unfolds the story of our world. However, the task of telling Earth's story is a challenging one. We are sure that all the stages shown here happened—but, in some cases, exactly when they took place is still unclear. This means that some of the dates mentioned in this book are uncertain, too.

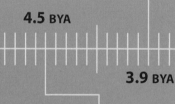

16: Earth cools

8: Cloud storm

12: Many worlds

20: Life evolves

4.65 BYA   **4.5** BYA   **3.8** BYA   **375** MYA

4.75 BYA   **4.6** BYA   **3.9** BYA   **500** MYA

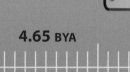

10: Sun birth

14: Moon birth

18: Life forms

KEY TO DATES:

BYA = billion years ago

MYA = million years ago

TYA = thousand years ago

YA = years ago

YIF = years into the future

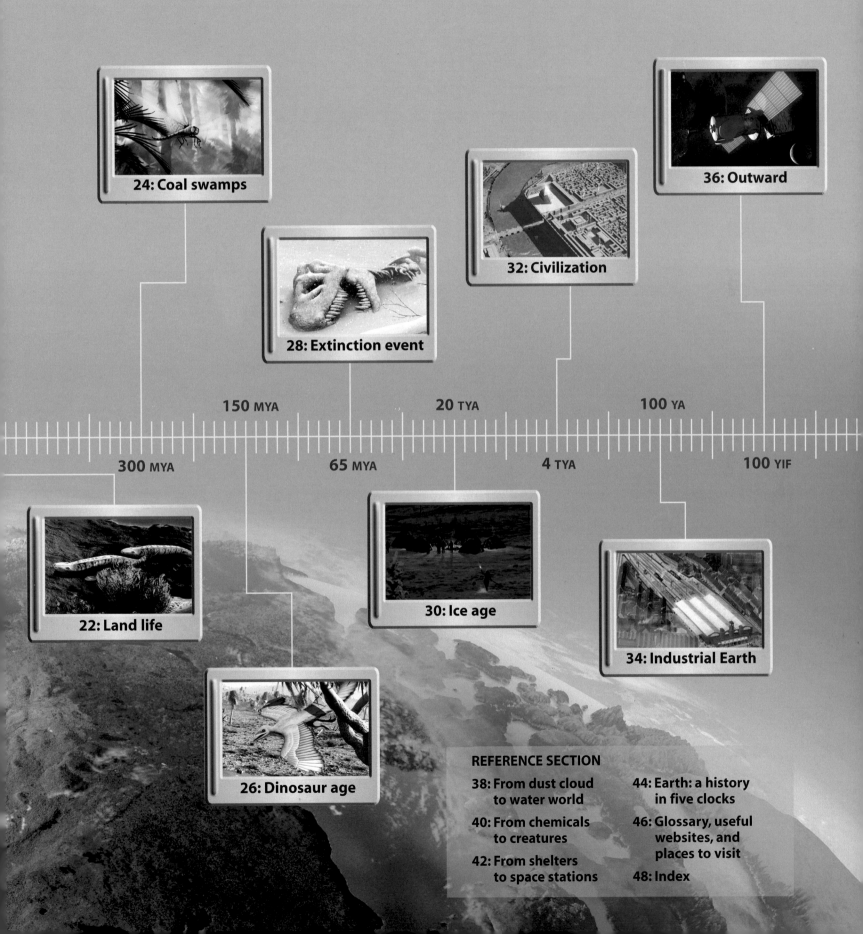

24: Coal swamps

28: Extinction event

32: Civilization

36: Outward

150 MYA

20 TYA

100 YA

300 MYA

65 MYA

4 TYA

100 YIF

22: Land life

30: Ice age

34: Industrial Earth

26: Dinosaur age

Cloud storm

4.75 billion years ago

A great dark cloud broods in space. It has been here for millions of years, occupying trillions of cubic miles, drifting in icy silence against a sparkling backdrop of stars. But the death of a nearby star, in the fiery turmoil of a supernova explosion, has sent shock waves surging through the cloud. The gas billows and twists, forming thicker, denser areas here and there. It is in one of these areas that Earth's past and future lie.

The solar system that includes Earth will form in this emerging proplyd (short for "protoplanetary disk")—the blob breaking away from the cloud.

Sun birth

Through the ceaseless, gentle tug of gravity, nearby cloud particles drift closer. The result is an area of increasing density and rising temperature. Finally, after tens of millions of years, this region of space begins to glow with heat and light. It becomes an infant star, the proto-Sun. Meanwhile, some of the nearby cloud material forms a vast, discus-shaped arrangement, with the proto-Sun at its center. Within it, lumps of ice and grit gather and grow.

Many worlds

4.6 billion years ago

Drifting lumps of matter collide and stick together. As they do so, the pull of their gravity increases, accelerating the collision of matter until some of the lumps are the size of small planets. But while some merge and grow, others are destroyed. As they orbit the newborn Sun, the young spheres sweep their paths clear of dust and gas, growing still larger as the infant solar system takes shape.

Moon birth

Few of the young planets were to survive for long. Many of them crashed into one another with such shattering impacts that they were smashed to pieces. But Earth is luckier. When it is struck by a planet, about one-third its size, it is only the smaller world that ends up being destroyed. The rubble that remains forms a great disk in orbit around Earth. Slowly, within the disk, gravity draws some of the fragments together once more, shaping them into the great globe of the Moon.

Earth's collision with a smaller, planetlike object causes huge amounts of debris to split off—enough to form a large moon.

Earth cools

3.9 billion years ago

Scarred by the impact of comets and great volcanic rifts, the surface of Earth is still hot from the forces of its creation. The fumes from fiery vents have given the planet an atmosphere that would be deadly to human beings and other modern life forms. But, slowly, the world is cooling down, and in roughly another 50 million years from the time of this scene, water vapor in the atmosphere will begin to condense (turn to liquid). All around the world, great rains will start to fall. Their waters will bring oceans to Earth.

Life forms

3.8 billion years ago

In Earth's shallow oceans, chemicals form and change in an endless variety of combinations. Strange, complex new molecules are made. They take in energy and other molecules, grow larger, and split to form copies of themselves. The copies make their own copies, and so their number grows rapidly. Different types appear, more complex still. They are able to move around and react to their immediate surroundings. In specks of jelly and clumps of slime, forms of life have appeared on Earth.

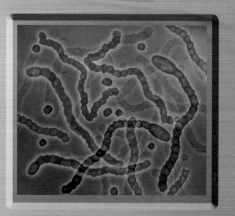

Living things like these, each only a fraction of a millimeter long, lived almost 3.5 billion years ago.

Life evolves

For millions of years, life spreads through the oceans of Earth. Though most offspring are identical to their parents, occasionally they are slightly different, and—in rare situations—these differences might give them an advantage: more speed or strength, or superior senses or defenses. These offspring have a better chance of surviving and breeding. Gradually, they replace the older forms until they, too, are replaced. This process of evolution produces a vast range of plants and animals, all struggling against one another for the limited supplies of food and space available. Most animals eat only plants, but some are ferocious predators that hunt and kill to survive.

Land life

While life thrived and fought in the oceans, the lands of the young Earth remained barren and uninhabited except for thin layers of slime on the rocks. Then, around 450 million years ago, more complex living things began to colonize the land, beginning with plants and insectlike creatures. These creatures left the ocean to find food, escape from enemies, or avoid the lack of oxygen in some coastal waters. Now, about 75 million years later, the smaller species that crawl and scurry around the shore are joined by larger beasts, lumbering landward on four legs. Four-limbed creatures will dominate the land from now on.

Coal swamps

Vast trees tower into the sky, their roots sucking moisture from the swampy ground, which is itself covered in a rich tangle of plant and animal life. This lush and dense vegetation produces a great deal of oxygen, creating the conditions that allow insects to grow to monstrous proportions. Huge dragonflies flap and flicker through the misty light, their shadows sweeping over scenes of vigorous life, violent death, and rapid decay. The dead remains of the swamp plants are covered and compressed by layers and layers of new growth until they are deeply buried. Long afterward, they will resurface again in the form of the coal reserves that will fuel the industrialization of Earth.

Dinosaur age

One highly successful group of reptilian animals now dominates the surface of Earth: the dinosaurs. The slow but certain process of evolution has colonized almost every part of the planet with forms of life, including the lower atmosphere. But the challenge of flight is far greater for large animals such as reptiles. At first, large airborne species could only flap and swoop clumsily. Then, about 150 million years ago, a strange creature called *Archaeopteryx* comes into existence. It has the claws and teeth of a reptile but the feathers of something quite new, exciting, and different: a bird.

Extinction event

For more than 100 million years, the dinosaurs and their kin were the unconquerable masters of Earth, dominating all other life forms on land, in the air, and under the sea. They might have been its masters still but for one world-changing event that occurred about 65 million years ago: a collision between this world and a smaller, airless one—an asteroid. The impact fills the whole atmosphere with thick dust, preventing much of the Sun's light and heat from reaching the planet's surface. In the endless, wintry twilight … the dinosaurs are dying out.

Ice age

These are testing times for life. Freezing weather has swept from the polar regions toward the equator, clasping much of the planet in an icy grip. Early humans are puny compared with the great beasts that roam the frozen wastes, and yet they survive the onslaught of ice. By learning to make fire and work together, they are able to defeat—and eat—animals much larger than themselves. So, while the peak of this most recent ice age spells death for the mammoth, the human species prospers, thanks to a unique combination of cunning, inventiveness, and teamwork.

Temporary shelters are made from materials that are easy to find and carry, such as branches, bones, tusks, and animal hides.

31

Civilization

Humans have found a new way of living.
Around 8000 BCE, people began to gather in permanent settlements. Small at first, some of them grew rapidly, becoming the first cities. There are many reasons for the success of such places: animals can be bred and crops can be grown nearby, making food supplies more reliable. Living in groups is safer, too. Cities also allow people to specialize in different activities, obtaining some things from others rather than producing everything for themselves. Thanks to city life, many new trades, skills, arts, and sciences have started to develop. Civilization has begun.

Industrial Earth

It is merely the blink of an eye compared with the vast age of Earth, but over just a few centuries, the planet is transformed as huge urban areas spread and sprawl across its face. Fueled by supplies of coal, oil, and gas laid down hundreds of millions of years ago, industrialization not only reshapes the world, it also damages it, contaminating the land, sea, and sky with waste and poison. But industrial technology brings huge benefits and advances in human knowledge, too—from new methods of transportation to the conquest of disease and the birth of new sciences.

Outward

100 years into the future

Earth's story is only half told. The Sun, on which all life depends, is in the middle of its own life. But it has billions of years left, and the planet should survive as long as its star does. Humans, in their determination to explore and expand, have already taken their first courageous steps into the wider universe, and this outward progress is likely to continue. We know that the Sun is not an unusual star: there are many like it, scattered like glittering dust throughout the universe. Many—perhaps most of them— have their own families of worlds. When Earth dies, in about five billion years, one of those worlds may become our second planet.

Old satellites, once miracles of technological achievement, become pieces of space junk that orbit Earth for centuries.

From dust cloud to water world

Words in **bold italics** are explained in the glossary (see pages 46–47).

The story of Earth begins about 4.75 billion years ago, in a great dark cloud of dust and gas, part of a large **galaxy** that Earth's inhabitants would one day name the Milky Way. At this time, the universe was about two-thirds its current age and size, having formed about nine billion years earlier in a mysterious event known as the **big bang**.

Cloud storm

4.75 billion years ago

Dark clouds usually drift silently through space with little activity in their cold depths, but this particular one had a different story. Suddenly, many billions of miles distant from the cloud, a pair of stars (or possibly a single star) exploded in a great flare of light and radiation, brighter than the whole Milky Way.

*We know little about conditions at this time. It may be that nearby stars were hot enough to form glowing gas clouds called **emission nebulae**.*

The sudden rush of energy into the dark cloud sent **shock waves** through it, disturbing its balance and sweeping its material into thicker regions here and there.

*A collapsing area of the cloud would one day be the site of the **solar system**, where Earth itself formed.*

Sun birth

4.65 billion years ago

Many of the thicker regions of the cloud collapsed under their own **gravity**. In their depths, the increasing **density** led to such high temperatures that these areas started to glow with light and heat, turning into **T Tauri stars**. One of these baby stars was the Sun.

The T Tauri star is glowing because of the heat generated by material falling into it. The star is highly active at this stage of its life and rotates much more quickly than it does when it gets older.

Many worlds

Around the young Sun, more cloud material formed (first) a disk. Then it created rings of material and (finally) many planets. Much more material remained as gas, dust, and rubble.

The continued collapse of the Sun eventually generated such internal heat that **nuclear fusion** began there, turning it into a **main sequence star**.

For many millions of years, the young solar system was an arena of planetary conflict, with many of the newly formed planets being destroyed in collisions with one another. Others merged, forming larger worlds— including our world: Earth.

There were about 30 planets in orbit around the Sun at this time.

Moon birth

One of the planets struck infant Earth with almost enough force to destroy it. But, instead, a great, cloudy disk of rock and dust was thrown up into orbit around the planet. Out of this disk of material, the Moon formed. It rapidly grew larger, sweeping up more material in its path along the rocky disk.

The Moon formed only a few tens of thousands of miles from Earth, but, as it slowed, its distance gradually increased. Its slow, outward spiraling continued from then on so that now it is more than ten times farther from us.

Earth cools

Gradually, Earth cooled down. While deep inside it was still glowing hot, a cooler, solid crust formed on its surface. Above the crust was an **atmosphere**, made up of gases captured by Earth's gravity and others expelled from its interior.

*The atmosphere of early Earth would have suffocated any of its present-day inhabitants. Made mainly of **methane**, it also contained **nitrogen**, **carbon dioxide**, and steam (boiling-hot water **vapor**).*

One day, almost a billion years after Earth's formation, the planet had become so cool that something happened that had never happened before: steam **condensed** in the upper atmosphere, and it began to rain. For millions of years, the rains fell, and water collected in the lowest parts of the crust. Slowly, Earth turned into a world of water as lakes became seas and seas joined together into great oceans covering most of the surface.

*Big impacts from **comets** and **asteroids** battered Earth, sending shock waves racing through land, sea, and air.*

From chemicals to creatures

Words in **bold italics** are explained in the glossary (see pages 46–47).

Life forms

3.8 billion years ago

In the warm oceans of cooling Earth, **molecules** of different substances reacted and changed, producing new structures. Some of these structures had the rare abilities to absorb other molecules and to make copies of themselves. Like today's **viruses**, these tiny structures stood at the threshold between life and nonlife.

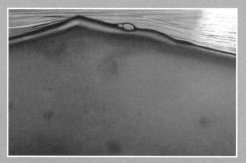

The sunlit waters near the surfaces of the ancient oceans were home to Earth's first living things.

Many different structures appeared, and the various types all multiplied until the oceans were filled with them. They began to run out of the molecules they needed, and the less effective ones ceased to multiply. The victories of the other types were short-lived: new, more complicated versions appeared and wiped out weaker forms until they, too, were replaced. In this way, things that we would recognize as living **cells** began to form and **evolve**.

Life evolves

500 million years ago

For more than three billion years, the dominant living creatures on Earth were tiny, jellylike cells that hardly changed at all over millions of years.

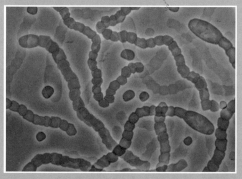

Microscopic creatures were responsible for changing Earth's atmosphere into one in which other life forms could thrive.

The process of change then speeded up, and many new types of living things appeared. Some of them had hard shells, which meant that their bodies left records in the rocks in the form of **fossils**. Thanks to these, we know a lot more about these creatures than we do about more ancient living things. To us, some of them would look very "alien," with spikes, claws, and pincers, eyes on stalks, and many flailing legs.

At about 3 ft. (1m) long, Anomalocaris was one of the largest creatures of its time.

Land life

For long ages, while the oceans swarmed with life, the land remained dead and barren. Eventually, primitive plant species took hold there, painting the landscape with new colors. Many millions of years later, a few animals began to explore the muddy shorelines, making brief forays onto land.

Tiktaalik *had lungs as well as simple legs, allowing it to survive in shallow water and to venture ashore.*

Over generations, **evolution** adapted their bodies until they had lungs that could breathe air rather than water, skins that did not dry out as quickly as those of their ancestors, and simple, stumpy legs. Their descendants would be even better suited to life on the land it was their destiny to conquer.

Coal swamps

300 million years ago

The struggle for existence continued on land as it did in the oceans. New species appeared and fought with the old for food and space. Vigorous plant growth laced the atmosphere with plentiful supplies of **oxygen**, and giant dragonflies flapped through the humid air of swamp forests, while monstrous spiders and scorpions scurried through the thick, tangled undergrowth. Huge **reptiles** and glistening **amphibians** wallowed in the warm, dark mud, waiting for their moment to devour their **prey**—or to be devoured themselves.

Meganeura, *a giant dragonfly with a wingspan of more than 30 in. (75cm)*

In the warm, damp conditions, dead creatures would have rotted away quickly—if they were not eaten by the **maggots** *of giant insects first.*

Dinosaur age

150 million years ago

The world was full of different environments, from thick jungles to hot deserts. Plants and animals lived in all of these places. Each **species** had adapted to survive in the conditions it found in its environment.

Compsognathus *was a small, flesh-eating dinosaur, probably closely related to* Archaeopteryx *(below).*

In many lands, dinosaurs evolved. Some were small and vicious **predators**, while others were large, placid beasts that browsed on the abundant plant life—and some were giant, ferocious killers. From dinosaurs, the first birds evolved. They were poor, awkward fliers at first but fiercely competitive in their attempts to conquer the new world of the air.

Archaeopteryx *had wings and feathers like a bird but teeth and claws like a dinosaur. It could climb trees and glide down from them but may not have been able to take to the air from the ground like most modern birds.*

From shelters to space stations

Words in **bold italics** are explained in the glossary (see pages 46–47).

Extinction event

65 million years ago

The dinosaurs were the most successful creatures that have ever lived on the planet, dominating Earth for more than 100 million years. But when a huge comet or asteroid collided with the planet, it raised a worldwide dust cloud, cutting off the Sun's light. The dinosaurs were unable to cope with the rapidly plunging temperatures, and all of them perished. Many other species died out, too, but a few prospered—including our own mouselike ancestors.

Because they were so small, early mammals needed little food to survive. Their body chemistry and dense fur helped them keep the cold at bay.

These **mammals** proved to be a very successful type of animal. They were **warm-blooded**, so they could survive in low temperatures as long as they could find food. They also protected their young and even trained them. Gradually, the succeeding generations became more intelligent.

Ice age

20,000 years ago

The control of fire was a very important achievement, giving these early people protection, warmth, light at night, and the ability to cook their food.

Earth itself underwent periodic climate changes, with warm periods interrupted by frigid **ice ages**. By the most recent of these ice ages, several humanlike mammal species had evolved. These new species were highly intelligent and equipped with hands that combined the strength and delicacy required to make tools and weapons. They were also social, with the ability to work together. These attributes meant that they could defeat even animals much larger than themselves.

Weapons, flaming torches, and loud shouts were all used in life-or-death contests with large or dangerous prey.

Civilization

Of all the humanlike species, our own kind—called **Homo sapiens**—were unbeatable. Over the space of only a few thousand years, they spread across most of Earth. Though they began as a race of hunters, they later learned the benefits that can come from staying in the same place. They began to settle in fertile areas, where they built towns and cities in the midst of large areas of organized farmland.

Strong city walls provided security for those inside. A network of water channels provided **irrigation** for the farmland areas outside the city walls.

This shows an ancient temple. Religion helped give early civilizations a social structure, a moral code of behavior, and a sense of identity for their people.

Industrial Earth

Humans learned to study their world, and the discovery of science helped them unlock its secrets. Through science came technology, giving the human race control over all other species and the power to remake the landscape and travel rapidly across the planet. They also had the power to destroy, through great wars and through **pollution**. Humans have used all their powers to the full. As a result, human history is marked by global conflict and destruction but also by great strides in knowledge, exploration, and the quest for peace.

A web of railroads appeared across the globe, thanks to steam-powered technology, rapid advances in **metallurgy**, and the vast numbers of manual workers needed to install this important new **infrastructure**.

Outward

In the final few decades of the 20th century—a mere heartbeat in the overall lifetime of Earth—human beings left their own world for the first time and began their exploration of the boundless universe.

Space stations, powered by sunlight, became the first human settlements in space. In the future, there might be larger space cities, glowing in the sky.

In a few billion years, the Sun will start to run out of **hydrogen** and grow vast, melting the surface of our world and perhaps swallowing it up entirely. But that might not be the end of the story. The inhabitants of Earth—who might be human beings or some other, more advanced species—may have learned to conquer space as our ancestors learned to conquer the seas and then the whole planet. If so, they could spread to other **star systems**, and new stories may begin on new Earths, under new suns.

Space is vast, but so is the power of human ingenuity. Here, a spacecraft leaves Earth to explore new worlds.

Earth: a history in five clocks

A thousand years is an immense distance in time. Imagine how the area around your home might have looked that long ago, and how alien and different it would seem if you visited it. Yet the birth of the ancient planet on which we live took place millions of times further back than this—an unimaginable gulf of years.

For the past few billion years, Earth has been an inhabited world, but for much of that time, the development of its occupants has been very slow. Once the human species began to evolve, the pace of change got faster, and with each millennium (1,000 years) that has passed, more and more changes have occurred. So, in this book—as in any other history of the world—time seems to move faster as the pages turn.

These five "clocks" represent periods of time. Each one represents just 1 percent of the clock to its left. From left to right, these diagrams show the entire age and history of the universe, and at what stages Earth and its living things became a part of it.

Clock one

The past 14,000,000,000 years

Time, like Earth, has an age: it has existed for 13.7 billion years since it, together with space and energy, came into existence in a sudden and mysterious event called the big bang. The rapid expansion of space that began then has continued ever since.

Clock two

The past 140,000,000 years

The patterns of the **continents** and oceans of Earth have shifted and changed, and our world has been blasted by asteroids and frozen by repeated ice ages. Many types of living creatures have evolved and changed, too, as new **habitats** became available on the developing planet.

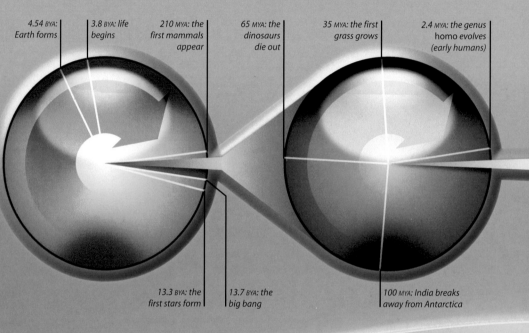

4.54 BYA: Earth forms

3.8 BYA: life begins

210 MYA: the first mammals appear

65 MYA: the dinosaurs die out

35 MYA: the first grass grows

2.4 MYA: the genus homo evolves (early humans)

13.3 BYA: the first stars form

13.7 BYA: the big bang

100 MYA: India breaks away from Antarctica

7 BYA •

13.7 BYA: the big bang

13.3 BYA: the first stars form
•

KEY:
BYA = billion years ago
MYA = million years ago
TYA = thousand years ago
BCE = before common era (BC)
CE = common era (AD)

Clock three

The past 1,400,000 years

The past 1.4 million years have seen the gradual evolution of the human species and its spread across the planet. The combination of intelligence, hands that can grasp tools and build, and the ability to work together have been keys to the success of this species.

Clock four

The past 14,000 years

Over the past 14,000 years, human beings have changed the face of Earth, turning huge areas into farmland, peppered with settlements that range from tiny villages to great cities.

Clock five

The past 140 years

For the past 140 years, the development of industrial technology has transformed the lives and lands of people throughout Earth, and the progress of science has finally taught us how tiny our planet is and how short our stay on it has been.

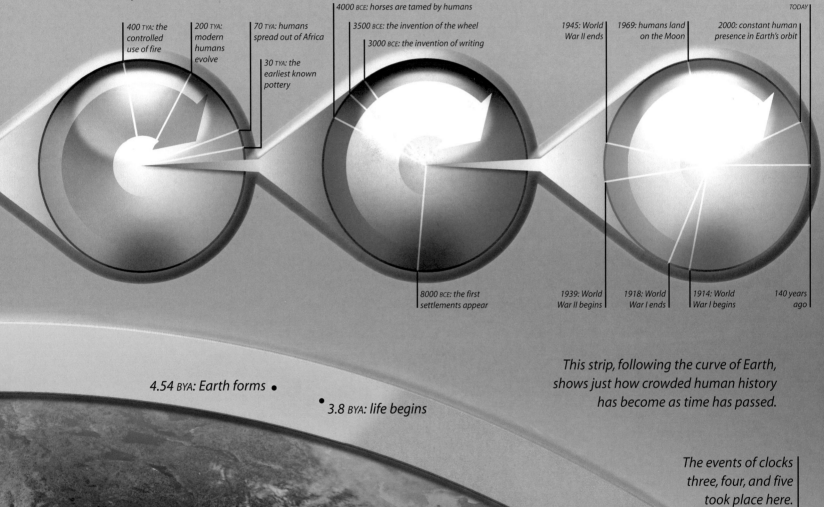

400 TYA: the controlled use of fire

200 TYA: modern humans evolve

70 TYA: humans spread out of Africa

30 TYA: the earliest known pottery

4000 BCE: horses are tamed by humans

3500 BCE: the invention of the wheel

3000 BCE: the invention of writing

8000 BCE: the first settlements appear

1945: World War II ends

1969: humans land on the Moon

2000: constant human presence in Earth's orbit

TODAY

1939: World War II begins

1918: World War I ends

1914: World War I begins

140 years ago

4.54 BYA: Earth forms •

• 3.8 BYA: life begins

This strip, following the curve of Earth, shows just how crowded human history has become as time has passed.

The events of clocks three, four, and five took place here.

The events of clock two took place here.

210 MYA: first mammals •

140 MYA

Today

Glossary

Words in **bold italics** refer to other glossary entries that you will find on these two pages.

amphibian
A type of animal that begins its life in the water but is later able to live on land.

asteroid
A small, airless world in **orbit** around the Sun.

atmosphere
A layer of gases around a **planet**.

atom
A basic unit of matter: the smallest **particle** of a chemical **element**.

big bang
The event that marks the beginning of the known universe.

carbon dioxide
A gas that animals breathe out and that plants take in.

cell
Every living thing is made up of one or more cells.

chemical
A substance in which groups of **atoms** are joined together in a repeating pattern.

comet
A large lump of grit and ice that travels on a long **orbit** (around the Sun) through the **solar system**.

condensed
Something has condensed when it has "changed state" from being a gas to being a liquid.

continent
A large land mass on the surface of Earth.

density
The amount of **mass** contained within a particular volume (a three-dimensional space).

element
A pure substance that cannot be made any simpler than it is.

emission nebula
A cloud of glowing gas in space.

evolution
The process by which living things gradually change (evolve) over many generations to become suited to their immediate environments.

extinction
The dying out of a specific type of living thing, then known as "extinct."

fossil
The remains of an ancient living thing, found in rock.

galaxy
A large group of stars and other material, held together by **gravity**.

gravity
The invisible force of attraction between objects in the universe, created by the **mass** of those objects. The Moon **orbits** Earth because Earth is more massive.

habitat
An area in which a particular type of plant or animal lives.

Homo sapiens
The Latin name, or **species** name, for today's human beings.

hydrogen
The lightest **element** and the most commonly occurring one in the known universe.

ice age
A period, lasting for thousands of years, during which Earth's average temperature is low.

infrastructure
The underlying, supporting structure that is required to make a system work properly.

irrigation
Watering plants artificially, using machines or channels.

maggot
The young, immature form of an insect.

main sequence star
A star that shines by converting **hydrogen** into helium. The Sun is a main sequence star.

mammal
An animal that is **warm-blooded**, with hair or fur, and that feeds on its mother's milk when it is young.

mammoth
An **extinct** type of **mammal** related to modern elephants and that often had long hair and tusks.

mass
The amount of matter (stuff) that something contains. The mass of objects is what creates the effects of **gravity**.

metallurgy
The study of metals and how to use them—for example, in jewelry, industry, and manufacturing.

methane
A gas made of the *elements hydrogen* and carbon. It burns when in the presence of *oxygen*.

molecule
A group of two or more *atoms*, held tightly together.

nitrogen
The gas that makes up most of Earth's *atmosphere* today.

nuclear fusion
A process in which light *atoms* join together to make heavier ones, releasing energy as they do so.

orbit
The path of one object around another in space, created by their *gravity*.

oxygen
A gas in Earth's *atmosphere* that human beings need to breathe.

particle
A tiny part of something. *Molecules* and *atoms* are particles.

planet
A large world in *orbit* around the Sun or another star.

pollution
Something that damages or disturbs living things by affecting the land, sea, or air they live in or on. Industrial pollution has been adding *carbon dioxide* to Earth's *atmosphere*, which contributes to global warming.

predator
An animal that kills and eats other animals in order to survive.

prey
An animal killed by another for food.

reptile
A type of animal that is cold-blooded and covered in scaly skin.

shock wave
A sudden pulse of energy that travels rapidly through a solid, liquid, or gas.

solar system
The Sun, its orbiting *planets*, and other objects that travel around it.

species
A particular type of animal or plant. Usually, members of a particular species breed only with one another.

star system
A star, its *planets*, and the other objects that go around the star.

supernova
A huge explosion in space, produced by the collapse of a single star or a sudden change in a pair of stars.

T Tauri star
A type of young star in which *nuclear fusion* has not yet started.

vapor
A gas that can easily be changed into a liquid through a process known as *condensation*.

virus
A tiny, microscopic organism that behaves like a complex *chemical* in some ways and a living thing in others. Viruses need to use the *cells* of living things to reproduce themselves.

warm-blooded
A warm-blooded animal has a certain kind of body chemistry that means it can keep the temperature of its blood constant. This means that it can survive in cold conditions.

Useful websites
Look online to see images of Earth from space and to follow its story.

BBC's History of Life on Earth
www.bbc.co.uk/nature/history_of_the_earth

NASA's Planetary Photojournal
http://photojournal.jpl.nasa.gov/targetFamily/Earth

National Geographic's Prehistoric Time Line
http://science.nationalgeographic.com/science/prehistoric-world/prehistoric-time-line

Natural History Museum, London, U.K.: Earth pages
www.nhm.ac.uk/nature-online/earth/index.html

Places to visit
Visit these inspiring places to discover more about the evolution of Earth, see the fossils that teach us about the past, and marvel at new technology.

American Museum of Natural History
Central Park West at 79th Street
New York, NY 10024
(212) 769-5100
www.amnh.org

Lawrence Hall of Science
One Centennial Drive
Berkeley, CA 94720
(510) 642-5132
http://lawrencehallofscience.org

Saint Louis Science Center
5050 Oakland Avenue
Saint Louis, MO 63110
(314) 289-4400
www.slsc.org

Index